EXPLORERS WANTED!
In the Desert
Simon Chapman

EXPLORERS WANTED!

books by Simon Chapman

Simon Chapman
EXPLORERS
WANTED!

In the Desert

LITTLE, BROWN AND COMPANY

New York ⌁ Boston

Little, Brown and Company

Time Warner Book Group
1271 Avenue of the Americas, New York, NY 10020
Visit our Web site at www.lb-kids.com

First U.S. Edition: January 2006

First published in Great Britain by Egmont Books Limited in 2004

Library of Congress Cataloging-in-Publication Data

Chapman, Simon, 1965-
    In the desert/by Simon Chapman.
        p. cm.— (Explorers wanted!)
    ISBN 0-316-15545-4
    1. Natural history—Sahara—Juvenile literature. 2. Sahara—Description and
travel—Juvenile literature. I. Title

    QH195.S3C49 2005
    916.604—dc22

                                                            2004063297

10 9 8 7 6 5 4 3 2 1

COM-MO

Printed in the United States of America

CONTENTS

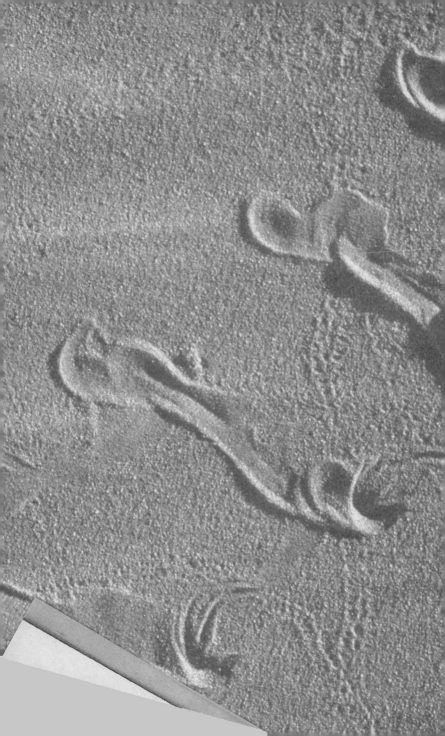

SO...YOU WANT TO EXPLORE THE SAHARA DESERT?

You want to...

Traverse the endless **dunes** by camel?

Drink your fill in a **sparkling oasis**?

Meet the **foreign people** and **strange creatures** that inhabit this arid wasteland?

If the answer to any of these questions is **YES**, then this is the book for you. Read on...

THIS BOOK GIVES YOU the essential lowdown on life in this land of extremes, from how to cope with the intense heat and burning sun to **where you might find water** when at first glance there appears to be none. There'll also be the stories of some of the people who came before you, how they survived (or didn't!) in this, the greatest desert on Earth.

YOUR MISSION...

should you choose to accept it, is to get to the Ahaggan massif. Beyond the miles of flat gravel pans, the rocky *hammada*, and the great sand sea of Najmer stands a huge slab of rock, sculpted over the centuries by wind-blown sand into fantastic pinnacles and deep gorges, which the sun's rays never reach. The Tuareg camel caravans of the deep desert have avoided the Ahaggan over the years. There was no water or food for their animals. It was too easy to lose yourself in the treacherous terrain. Until recently, that is...

Forced to shelter in the rocks by a sudden sandstorm, a group of nomads, separated from their caravan, made a startling discovery. WATER. Cool and fresh and lots of it. When they finally made it out of the sand sea and *hammada* rock fields, the men told stories of a lost canyon with a lake and even a waterfall.

Painted on the canyon's walls were figures of giraffes, hippos, and zebra, animals of the African plains, not the Sahara desert. Seeing the state the men were in when they were found, few believed their story, especially as they could not explain how to get back to the valley.

So what is the truth? Could there really be a waterfall in the desert? What about the rock paintings? Who drew them and when? This is what you've decided to find out. Getting there will be some adventure. How will you start?

DJELLA OASIS

WELL AT BILAN

SAND SEA OF NAJMER

AHAGGAN MASSIF

Time to set the scene . . .

The Sahara desert is HUGE...

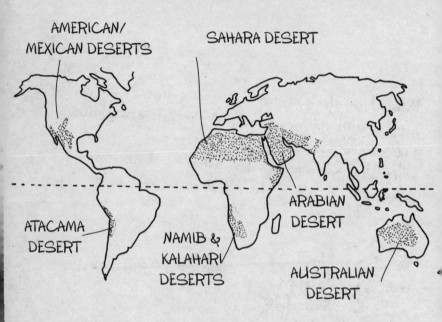

AMERICAN/
MEXICAN DESERTS

SAHARA DESERT

ATACAMA
DESERT

NAMIB &
KALAHARI
DESERTS

ARABIAN
DESERT

AUSTRALIAN
DESERT

It stretches right across the top of Africa, and other deserts
carry on beyond that through Arabia and the Middle East as
far as southern Pakistan and western India. Here it is hot,
dry, and parched. The ground is rocky or sandy, in some
places dotted with hardy plants that can endure the intense
heat and lack of water, in other places totally barren. The
Sahara and Middle East aren't the only hot deserts. If you
look at a map of the world you'll notice other deserts, like
the Namib and the Kalahari, mirrored across the equator in
southern Africa. And if you look at North and South America

you'll notice the same thing, desert in both north and south, jungle in between.

It's all to do with the way the sun heats the Earth. At the equator, hot air rises (it's called convection). Moist air from the oceans rushes in, so everything's wet and jungly. The air – with no moisture in it – falls at the Tropics of Cancer

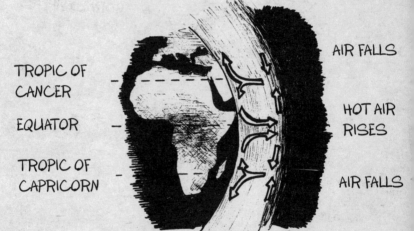

TROPIC OF
CANCER

EQUATOR

TROPIC OF
CAPRICORN

AIR FALLS

HOT AIR
RISES

AIR FALLS

and Capricorn. Those areas are deserts. Generally the winds blow away from there, taking away any moisture. So it's mostly cloudless, hot, and incredibly dry. But are all deserts the same?

Certainly many desert animals across the world have developed similar survival techniques ...

Take a look at this desert scene and the facts describing it. Remember, this book is about the Sahara. Which four descriptions are wrong for North Africa?

ONE-HUMPED CAMEL

CACTUS

JERBOA

1. Wild dromedary, one-humped camels.
2. Jerboa.
3. Nearly the entire desert is sandy.
4. It never rains.
5. Nighttime can be very cold.
6. Cactus.

Answers on page 8

ANSWERS from page 7

1. FALSE. All dromedaries in the Sahara are domesticated. The only place with wild one-humped camels is Australia (find out more in Chapter 5).

2. TRUE. It may look like a mini-kangaroo, and it hops like one, but it is a common Sahara rodent.

3. FALSE. Only fifteen percent is sand dunes, areas called *ergs*. The rest is gravel pans, *reg*, or rock outcrops, *hammada*.

4. FALSE. Rainfall is rare but does happen over the winter. Sometimes there are flash floods. The driest desert in the world is the Atacama Desert in South America, where there are places in which rain has never been known to fall.

5. TRUE. It can get down to around freezing (0 degrees Celsius) at night in the winter.

6. FALSE. Cacti live in America, though there are similar-looking prickly, water-storing plants in Africa called euphorbias.

What's it like in the Sahara?

Midday, the sun beats down. It's like being under a grill. The baked-hard earth underneath is radiating heat, too. A grill from above and below!

All around you the land is featureless and flat. There is no shade. Heat hazes make the horizon shimmer with mirages; the layers of heated air reflect the sky above, giving the illusion of water hanging just above ground level.

There is no sign of life. None at all. You can see no plants among the stones and hard earth at your feet, and if there are animals, they are hidden underground.

Your mouth feels parched. You keep sipping at your water bottle. It's nearly empty now. You know you must be sweating, yet your skin feels dry. The heat makes any liquid evaporate straight away. You're standing still, not even doing anything, and you're losing water seemingly as fast as you're drinking it. You feel you will overheat soon.

These two factors, the scorching sun and the lack of water, will affect all your decisions. For anything to survive out here, it has to be well adapted. It must be able to get water wherever it can and then retain that water. It must be able to cope with the intense heat, or avoid the problem by taking refuge underground.

You are not adapted for this environment, but don't take it personally. People are not adapted for life in the desert. And **you** don't just have to survive. **You** have to cross the gravelly *reg*, the rocky *hammada,* and the sandy *erg.* You will have to find out how the people who live in the deep desert, like the Tuareg nomads, cope. How do they thrive in conditions that would kill you within a couple of days?

You thought it was going to be easy? If you thought it was going to be all soft sand dunes, or traveling on flat land, think again! Only part of the Sahara is like that. The rest is rock and scrub and mountains. You'll have to scale the rocks of the Ahaggan massif and know how to deal with sandstorms and — rather weirdly for the desert — sudden flash floods. You'll need training and you'll need to be equipped.

Chapter 1

WHAT TO TAKE AND HOW TO STAY ALIVE

Huge and sandy with fantastically sunny weather, you could be forgiven for thinking that the Sahara is just one gigantic beach. But would you wear the same gear?

Choose an outfit from this pile of clothing that you think would be suitable for desert wear.

Head:

HAT 1   HAT 2   HAT 3

Body:

SLEEVELESS VEST   T-SHIRT   BAGGY SHIRT

Legs:

SHORTS   LONG LIGHTWEIGHT PANTS   JEANS

Feet:

SANDALS   LIGHTWEIGHT BOOTS WITH SOCKS

Now work out your score.

Item of clothing	Score	
hat 1	0	Your head is uncovered.
hat 2	1	No sun protection for the back of your head.
hat 3	2	Protection for front, back, and top.
vest	0	A good way to get badly sunburned shoulders.
T-shirt	1	Better, but no arm or neck protection.
baggy shirt	2	Sun protection and baggy so that air can circulate.
shorts	1	No sun protection below knee but cool.
jeans	1	Far too hot.
long pants	2	Same reasons as baggy shirt.
sandals	1	Good for evenings, but in the day your feet could get badly sunburned.
light boots with socks	2	Good choice. The socks will absorb your sweat and hopefully stop the boots rubbing against your feet.

Answers on page 14

Your Score

So why don't you dress as if you're going to the beach? Surely wearing very little would keep you cool.

It does . . . but at a cost. The reason why we humans sweat is because when water evaporates it takes energy to turn it from liquid into gas. And that energy is taken from your body. You cool down. So wear nothing in the desert, sweat, let it evaporate and stay cool. No problem . . . except, think about it, if you keep sweating, you keep losing water. And if you lose water you dehydrate . . . you die (well okay, you feel lousy, lose coordination and consciousness first, but the end result is the same — death).

Also, if you wear next to nothing, think SUNBURN. Okay, you can wear sunblock, but what SPF (Sun Protection Factor) would you need?

Stay out in the midday Sahara sun and you'll end up scarlet like a freshly cooked lobster before you can say "Tassili n'Ajjer, Erg de Tenere." Go for at least SPF 50 for your sunblock!

Consider what the Bedouin Arabs of the eastern Sahara wear: loosely flowing robes so air can circulate. Some sweat evaporates, but not too much liquid is lost.
Kaffia cloth and agal rope headgear keep out the sun and can be wrapped around to keep the sand and dust out. Light color reflects the sun's infra-red (heat) rays.

BEDOUIN

So why then do many Tuareg in the southern Sahara wear dark blue? Why indeed? Dark colors absorb heat most. Though the one thing that can be said for dark colors is that they radiate heat best, too.

Other things that will be useful:

- Sunglasses – if you don't have these, painting black under your eyes cuts down the glare. If you see desert people wearing what looks like black eyeshadow, this could be the reason why (of course, it could also be just for reasons of fashion or appearance).

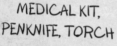

MEDICAL KIT, PENKNIFE, TORCH

SUNBLOCK

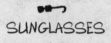

SUNGLASSES

IODINE

SLEEPING BAG

WATER BAG

PLASTIC SHEET

COOKING GEAR

EYESHADOW KIT

SPARE CLOTHES

WATER BOTTLE

- Water containers, bottles, or bags – VITAL. Carry several water containers. You'll need to drink a lot each day; and this being a desert, fresh drinking water will be hard to find.
- Iodine – two drops added to a liter of water will kill germs in impure water that are likely to give you an upset stomach. You'll have to get used to the foul taste it gives the water though (packets of powdered fruit drink or a squirt of lemon help).
- Spare clothes – for the evening. Sandals, shorts and T-shirt, a fleecy top in case the nights get cold, and sleeping bag.
- A plastic sheet is always useful – as an instant sunshade and as a water trap (you'll find out how to make one later).
- Cooking gear and some food (hopefully you'll be able to get hold of some along the way – see Chapter 5).
- Medical kit, penknife, torch (general exploration kit).
- Insect repellent. If you end up riding a camel across the desert, you won't be the only passenger. There'll be lots of fleas and ticks. Also, there will be mosquitoes and biting flies at water holes.

So keep cool, keep covered up, and keep hydrated (filled up with water).

This is what happens if you don't...

Dreadful Dangers of Heat and Sun

Sunburn. More than just being red and uncomfortable; we're talking about you getting genuine burns on your skin unless it is protected.

Dehydration. To start with, you may have headaches and no be able to concentrate well (your brain is seventy-five percent water). You'll stop feeling hungry. You will become constipated. Your pee will become concentrated and dark yellow (prolonged dehydration can lead to urine/kidney infections). As you become more dehydrated, you skin will look ashen-grey; your eyes will loc sunken and have bags under them. You will become dizzy and confused. You will breathe more rapidly, and your body will lose th ability to regulate its temperature. This may lead to...

1. Heat exhaustion. This is caused by too much exertion, making your body sweat out too much water and salt. You feel awful, overtired, and giddy. You may get muscle cramps.

OR . . .

2. Heatstroke (also called sunstroke). This is very serious. Your body is unable to keep its temperature at its regular 37 degrees Celsius. Sweating stops and you overheat. Your skin gets flushed and red. You have severe headaches, lose coordination, and may become confused and aggressive. Unless your body is cooled down, you'll have fits and die.

So, what do you do if you get any of these conditions? And the chances are you will, as you're going to be exploring (which is physically tiring) in a very hot place where there is very little water . . .

Match the treatment with the health condition

Health Condition	Treatment
1. sunburn	A. cover up and use sunscreen.
2. heatstroke	B. rest patiently in a cool, shaded place; drink fluids.
3. dehydration	C. drink lots of water, don't overexert yourself, eat some salt.
4. heat exhaustion	D. drink lots of water, don't overexert yourself.

Answers on page 22

These are rough guidelines only. On your trip into the Sahara you may suffer from a combination of these. Avoid this by drinking regularly, eating plenty of salt with your food, and not overdoing it.

How much water do you need?

In a hot desert climate, you need to drink at least six liters a day — and that's just for staying still in the shade. You'll need at least an extra half-liter for every hour that you're active, more if you exert yourself. Ten liters a day might be a sensible amount to allow yourself. Ten liters weighs ten kilograms, and of course you'll use up more water if you try carrying all of that...

How do you retain fluids?

Avoid water being *sweated, peed* (urinated), or *breathed out*.

A. Avoid exercise.

B. Breathe through your nose, not your mouth — and avoid talking.

C. Keep Cool, stay in shade.

D. Don't Drink coffee or coke — these drinks contain diuretic chemicals that make you pee more often.

E. Don't Ever lie on hot ground.

Which ways of keeping water in your body match with **sweated, peed** (urinated), or **breathed out**?

Answers on page 22

ANSWERS from page 20

1. A   2. B   3. D   4. C

ANSWERS from page 21

sweated: A, C, and E   *urinated:* D   *breathed:* B

Note: If you really have to survive without water, don't eat since your body needs water to digest food. Certainly don't drink alcohol or smoke.

So, it all comes down to the fact that in the desert, if you are going to survive you are going to need to be able to find water. And if that's not possible, you will need to carry it. At ten liters a day, that's going to add up to some weight you've got with you. It's clear you're going to need transportation.

How about using a wheelbarrow?

Geoffrey Howard did when he crossed the Sahara in 1974. He pushed a special Chinese sailing wheelbarrow from Beni Abbes, in Algeria, to Kano, in Nigeria. The design featured an enormous wheel, which easily went over the bumps in the road but was narrow and had the unfortunate habit of sinking deep into the sand at the roads' edges whenever the huge wheelbarrow was blown off-course. Howard also had some well-thought-out clothing for the trip – a huge cotton shirt and a tall straw hat with a hole in the top for ventilation, clothes normally worn by Fulani cattle herders in the southern Sahara.

Geoffrey Howard's trip was tough. He needed two soldiers in a Land Rover for backup. You don't have this. It's clear you're going to need a plan.

Chapter 2
HUGE HOT EMPTINESS

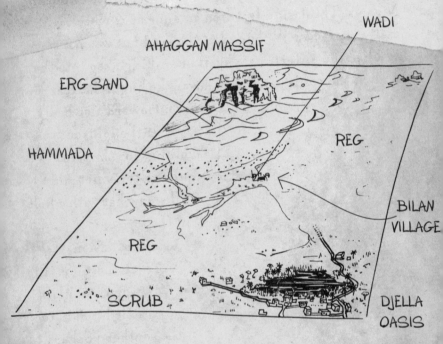

WADI

AHAGGAN MASSIF

ERG SAND

HAMMADA

REG

REG

BILAN
VILLAGE

SCRUB

DJELLA
OASIS

To make your journey, you'll have to plan your route around
where you can get water and how you can best travel over the
terrain that faces you. Here's a rough map of what lies ahead.
It's only accurate close to the start of your journey.
Remember, few have been to the Ahaggan plateau, so the map
is less accurate the further you go into the desert.

These are the three types of desert ahead of you.

· **Reg.** Gravel plains. Flat and open with few large rocks. Firm ground.
· **Erg.** Sand dunes. Steep slopes in places with soft sand that may slide easily.
· **Hammada.** Rock fields. Firm ground strewn with boulders.

REG   HAMMADA   ERG

Transportation options: this table shows whether or not you can travel on the various types of terrain.

Transport Option	Reg	Erg	Hammada
Truck	Yes – fast	Yes – though very difficult	No
Walking	Yes – slowly	Yes – slowly	Yes – slowly
Camel	Yes	Yes	Yes – slowly

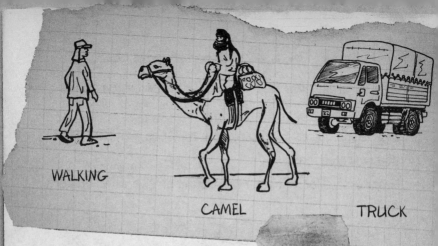

WALKING

CAMEL

TRUCK

Water sources:
- Djella **oasis**
- The **well** at Bilan
- **Wadi?**
- A **pool** in a gorge: Ahaggan plateau — unknown location

Use the information on the previous page and above to answer these questions about your route.

1. What sort of transportation is most suitable at the start?
2. Where should you make your first stop?
3. Which area will it be difficult to travel to by truck?
4. Which area will it be impossible to travel to by truck?
5. What is the most suitable way to travel across the erg?
6. Where is the only place that walking with pack animals (like donkeys) is the best option?

Answers are on page 35

There are plenty of trucks at the Djella oasis. With its date palms and rough pasture for sheep and goats, there's a thriving market. Traders from the coast bring in manufactured goods (anything from plastic pots to televisions) in exchange for the agricultural produce of the oasis. This is just the sort of place to stock up on extra provisions: dried apricots and dates, couscous (crushed semolina wheat), and lentils for easy-to-carry trail rations. There is also, of course, lots of fresh water (at a price!) for you to fill up your water containers.

As far as the traders are concerned, Djella is the edge of the wilderness. They rarely travel any deeper into the desert. There's just not enough profit in taking their goods to the scattered villages and nomads in the dried-up river valleys (wadis) before the great erg. That is, unless you are willing to pay to make it worth their while. . . . After some haggling, you cut a deal. Mohamed Ibrahim will do the run to the well at Bilan.

Perhaps you paid him too much, you decide a few minutes later when you see how happy he looks as he loads boxes of videos, plastic plates, and cans of meat onto the back of his truck. Once that's done and the truck is filled to overflowing, Mohamed drives round Djella several times picking up passengers (fee-paying, of course) who also want to come to Bilan. You realize that these passengers have come from Bilan to go to the market at Djella. The thought strikes you that surely they had arranged their transportation back home. Maybe they already had. That's why Mohamed looks so pleased.

The terrain outside Djella is semi-desert rather than being totally lifeless and barren. There are withered tufts of grass and gnarled, stunted bushes which look like they've had more than their fair share of nibbling from the flocks of goats you see from time to time. But, after you've left the immediate area of the oasis, there are no more date palms and there are no more trees. There simply isn't enough water for trees to survive. Life is tough for any plant living out here: very little water and intense dry heat. How do they survive?

LIFE AS A DESERT SURVIVOR!

Roots

· Soak up as much water as possible as soon as it rains with wide-spreading roots.

· Grow really deep (a hundred meters if necessary) to get down to underground water.

· Store water where it won't get dried up by the sun.

Stems

· Stay short. There's no point in growing taller than your neighbors. There are none around to "shade you out." There is plenty of sunlight to go round.

· Store water in your stem.

Leaves

· Stop water evaporating.

· Be small or spiny.

· Have a waxy coating.

· Cut down on your stomata — the holes in the leaf allowing gases from the air to get in and out for photosynthesis — OR have stomata that automatically close when it gets too hot.

QUIZ

Look at these two Saharan plants. Check which features you think each has.

Plant	Leaves	Stem	Roots
thorny mimosa bush	small and waxy/needle	short/water-storing	deep/wide
euphorbia	small and waxy/needle	short/water-storing	deep/wide

Important point about euphorbias

Though they may look like cacti, do not under any circumstances think you can get a drink by cutting into them and taking a sip (not even a good idea with most cacti). Euphorbia sap is thick, white, poisonous, and caustic — it will "burn" your mouth. Even using dried-up euphorbia stems as firewood is a bad idea. People have died after eating meat roasted over a euphorbia fire!

EUPHORB

MIMOSA

What about the grass you see in fairly evenly spaced clumps? How does that survive? What you can see looks yellow and dead. Is it? *NO.* Parts of the roots are alive. This is why …

An alternative strategy to desert life

Live out your whole cycle when it rains!
Spend the rest of the time under the soil as a bulb or a seed. When it rains, sprout, grow up, flower, and spread your seeds really quickly (a few days) before the sand has totally dried out. Make sure your flowers are really bright with lots of sugary nectar to attract all those insect pollinators.

Carrying on …

It's not long out of Djella before what passes for a road gives out entirely. Not that it really matters. The land is pancake-flat — faint tracks in the dirt show where vehicles have passed before. In the tire treads are strands of dead grass. Sometime when it last rained, the tracks held water just long enough for dormant seeds in the dirt to germinate. You also notice movement in some of the deeper tracks — yellow-brown

insects. Grasshoppers? Locusts.
This is just a "small" band
of several hundred
wingless hoppers
bunched together, sheltered
from the wind … but what
happens when this bunch meet more of their
kind and grow up? Then you have a …

LOCUST SWARM

Here's how it works:

· Bands of desert locusts arrive with the incoming winds.
  They need bare, wet earth to lay their eggs on. They are
  relying on the wind bringing rain. The plants that will then
  spring up will provide food for the hatching
  hoppers. Usually the rainclouds
  simply pass by,
  but if rain
  falls and
  everything
  goes as
  planned (for the
  locusts, that is) …

- The eggs hatch and the young wingless hoppers have plenty of fresh young shoots to feed on. They form into bands, chomping their way forward across the vegetation.

- The locusts grow bigger, shedding their skins as they do so (by then a new larger exoskeleton has grown underneath). Now they cover more ground, perhaps a kilometer a day.

- On their final skin change, the locusts become adults with wings. Now the swarm can cover much more ground, perhaps fifty kilometers a day, devastating any vegetation along the way.

- By now the swarm may be as big as fifty kilometers wide. It's as if the mass of insects is rolling forward. A wave of locusts lands and starts chomping. The next wave lands ahead of them, then the next wave, and so on. When the first wave has run out of food, it "leapfrogs" over the others. The swarm rolls on, devastating anything growing in the way.

- Fertile grasslands are destroyed. Crops are ruined. Across the world in any year, the scourge of the desert locust affects millions of people.

But it's not all bad news. Locusts make good meals. In some parts of Africa, people see locust swarms as a food bonanza. Like any other meat, they are a good source of protein.

Some locust recipes

· Take off the legs and eat raw.
· Fry or boil, it's not unlike eating prawns.
· Or if you can't face the sight of insects on your dinner plate, dry your locusts and grind them into a paste. Then you can mix them with other foods, which disguises what you're actually eating.

Mohamed's truck trundles on; hour after monotonous hour of featureless plain. From time to time, passengers in the back of the truck bang on the window at the back of the cab. One time, one man clambers right around to the cab and shouts through the window at the driver. Mohamed seems determined not to stop. You notice the engine's temperature gauge on the dashboard is rising. Is that steam coming from under the hood? The engine's whining now. It doesn't sound good. Now you're slowing down, losing power.

When the truck finally freewheels to a stop, the people on the back eagerly jump off. They were desperate to go to the toilet. While they relieve themselves, you glance at Mohamed. He is staring with what looks like horror at the steam rising from the radiator. He turns the ignition key. Nothing happens. It is clear this truck is going nowhere.

You, Mohamed, and six passengers are stuck. Welcome to the Sahara desert. What will you do now?

ANSWERS from page 26

1. Truck. Faster over reg.
2. The well at Bilan.
3. Erg sand dunes.
4. Hammada.
5. Camel.
6. The wadi.

Chapter 3
NO WAY OUT

The situation. It's three in the afternoon on the endless flat of the gravel pan. You, Mohamed, and six passengers are alone, clustered in the shade around a broken-down truck. It is hot. Very hot. The warm breeze that wafts over the baking earth feels like a hair dryer.

You have some water, but it won't go very far between eight people. It depends on how long you stay out here.

What should you do?

There are really two options.

A. One or more of you sets off toward the Bilan village (Mohamed says it isn't far).

B. You all wait here and hope help will come. Maybe you can make a signal of some sort.

Here are advantages and disadvantages that go with options A and B.

Decide which statement goes with which option.

1. Your water supplies would last longer by staying put.
2. You would have to walk using a compass. In this vastness it would be easy to get it wrong and miss Bilan entirely.
3. Walking uses much more water.
4. You might never be found.

Make your decision. The right course of action to take is given on the next page. But first . . .

Isn't that water you can see ahead of you? The horizon seems to shimmer. It's hard to tell, but it looks like there's a lake over there in the distance. You can see the sunlight glinting off of it.
Water . . . and where there's water . . . cool drinks . . . shade . . . ice cream?

37

No. Get real. It's a mirage.

This is how it works:

The layers of air just above the ground are hotter than the air above and reflect an image of the sky to your eyes. What you see is not water glinting in the sun, but the bright sky shining at you.

But what about the ice-cream stall and lounge chairs? Sorry, they are just a figment of your overactive imagination.

Back to your decision; to go for help or not? You choose Option B.

Do not move. Stay where you are. A lone person in the desert

is so much harder to find than a large
truck. Even if you walked in the right
direction, the chances are you
could not carry enough water or
stay cool enough to walk to
safety. Even if you walked at night
when it's cooler, you probably
wouldn't make it. There are
many cases of vehicles
stranded in the desert whose
drivers have attempted to walk to safety and died.

This is one of those situations where doing nothing is
the best option.

Even though, in the boredom and frustration you will feel
in the hours ahead, you will think over your decision again
and again, stick by your choice.

By sundown, the temperature is rather pleasant. Your fellow passengers pull up some of the scrubby plants close to Mohamed's truck and build up a fire. They are chatty and good-humored. Being stuck out in the desert clearly does not bother them as much as it bothers you. They chat and tell stories well into the night, gradually edging closer and closer to the fire as the temperature drops even more.

Though it very rarely gets below freezing in the Sahara, the temperature can dip quite markedly during the night. The ground radiates heat and there's no cloud cover to reflect some of this heat back. In winter it could be a chilly 0 degrees Celsius at night, up to around 37 degrees (human body temperature — warm but not really scorching) in the day. Often it feels cold because of the wind blowing. It's in the summer that the temperature becomes oven-like (50 degrees C). Then it's cooler in the night, though nowhere near freezing.

You can use the temperature drop to make a dew trap. Hollow out a small pit, lay your plastic sheet over the top, and weigh it down with stones. The idea is that any moisture in the air condenses on the plastic. You might get yourself a small sip of water this way, though not the liters you'll need for the hot day ahead.

After dark. This is the time for all the other inhabitants of the desert to come out from their cool burrows and resume their everyday lives.

This is a food web showing some of the animals you might come across. Study it to work out who's eating who.

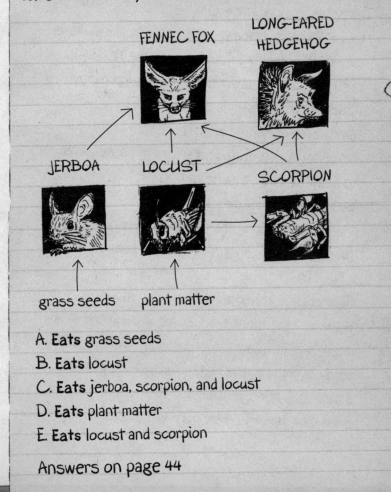

A. **Eats** grass seeds
B. **Eats** locust
C. **Eats** jerboa, scorpion, and locust
D. **Eats** plant matter
E. **Eats** locust and scorpion

Answers on page 44

These animals are all nocturnal. It makes a lot of sense to spend the day hidden in a shady burrow and only come out in the cool of the night. However, you still need to adapt to intense heat and lack of water.

Take the jerboa, for example...
- Large ears with blood vessels close to the surface for radiating heat away and cooling the blood (also pretty good for hearing the fennec fox coming; notice it has the same adaptation).
- Hardly ever pees, and when it does its urine is incredibly concentrated so as not to waste water.
- No need to drink. It gains all the moisture from the food it eats, either directly or when the food is broken down during the process of respiration (food + oxygen = energy released + carbon dioxide + WATER).
- Light color — reflects the sun's radiation.
- Burrows long tunnels under the ground and seals itself in to maintain a cool, constant climate until it's ready to come out at night. Because they have such small, weak arms, jerboas use their entire body — even their nostrils — for burrowing!

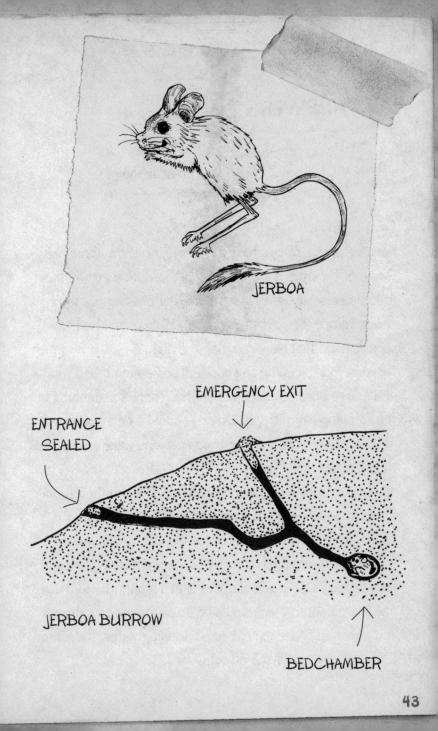

JERBOA

EMERGENCY EXIT

ENTRANCE
SEALED

JERBOA BURROW

BEDCHAMBER

A. jerboa	B. scorpion	C. fennec fox
D. locust	E. long-eared hedgehog	

First Light.

Huddled in your sleeping bag by the dying embers of the fire.
Some of the others are already up. You notice that as they
dress themselves, they make a point of shaking out their
shoes before they put them on. Why is this? Is it just to
remove sand that blew in during the night?

Down in your sleeping bag you feel something brush your
arm. You're sure it wasn't just an itch. There's something in
the sleeping bag with you. Oh no — could it be a scorpion?
That must have been why your companions were shaking out
their clothes and shoes.

You lie very still. No sudden moves now. Though the venom
from most Saharan scorpions is unlikely to kill you, you
could be temporarily paralyzed, or the shock, pain, and
swelling that a sting would give you might incapacitate you
for several days. Stuck out here with a broken-down truck
and limited water, there would be no chance for treatment.
You would just have to rest, keep drinking water, and sit (or
lie) out the worst of the effects.

Some say putting the blue blood of the scorpion that stung you on the wound may help, but that's unproven and in trying to kill your attacker you may end up getting another sting (even a dead scorpion can inject venom if you brush past its tail).

Or . . . you could cut the wound and suck out the poison, though that may lead to an even worse bacterial infection than the sting would have given you. Worse still, you might end up poisoning yourself through cuts or ulcers in your mouth.

Let's face it, if you get stung there's not a lot you can do. Wash the wound, stay calm, keep up your fluid levels, and rest. Scorpions are reasonably common in all areas of the Sahara, and scorpion stings are a part of life out here. They're just a fact you have to deal with in the desert of life.

Some scorpion facts

Scorpions are arachnids, like spiders. Their basic body design has remained unchanged for over a hundred million years.

Scorpions get all the liquid they need from sucking out the bodies of their prey — insects like locusts. This takes a few hours, leaving just an empty "shell."

Scorpions glow (fluoresce) greenish when put under ultraviolet light

So what do you do now?

Ever so slowly you start unzipping your sleeping bag and whistle to attract the attention of Mohamed, who's fiddling with the truck's engine (again). He comes over and flicks something off you with a bit of brushwood.

"Gam gam," he says, picking a harmless black beetle off the earth and chucking it to one side. It's not just scorpions that like to snuggle into the folds of your clothes while you are sleeping.

Later. *The sun's beating down. It's already very hot. Your patch of shade next to the truck is shrinking as the sun rises higher in the sky.*

This will be your second day of being stuck in the reg gravel pan. Surely your water will run out unless it's strictly rationed. So why do none of the others look concerned? They seem quite cheerful, chatting among themselves, occasionally pointing toward the southern horizon where a tiny, dirty smudge discolors the otherwise blue sky.

Why aren't the passengers worried?

Decide which statement is reasonable.

A. Surviving the desert is second nature to them. These hardened desert-dwellers can survive days in extreme heat without water.

OR...

B. They had told their families in Bilan when they would get
   back and know that someone will send a vehicle out to look
   for them if they don't return. You can see the dust cloud
   caused by that vehicle approaching.

OR ...

C. The dust cloud is a sandstorm in the distance. That means
   the weather will soon become cooler and cloudy.

Answers on page 50

By the end of the day you're in the wadi — the dried-up river
valley at Bilan — in Mohamed's truck! It had been very easy
for the driver of the second truck to repair it. Unlike
Mohamed, he had been prepared and brought a few simple
spare parts and a tool kit with him.

"Getting stuck in the desert is just an 'occupational
hazard'," Mohamed jokes. It's happened to him many times
before, but it always works out in the end ... "Or at least it
has so far," he adds quietly.

Tonight you will sleep in the back of the truck (let's hope it
will be scorpion-free). Tomorrow, Mohamed's sisters,
Fatiima and Assalama, will take you up the wadi to an
encampment of Tuareg desert nomads. Hopefully, they'll be
willing to take you on one of their camels across the great
sand erg to the mountains at Ahaggan.

Chapter 4
WATER. WATER.

To call Bilan a village would probably be going too far. It's more of a scattered collection of mud-brick houses and nomads' tents set along a shallow valley that, judging from the tidemark of brush and twigs along the sides, once held running water. There's some moisture still under the soil in the valley floor. There are clumps of bushes and even the odd, twisted acacia tree. You can see goats grazing and, close to where Mohamed parked his truck, a well. This is the center of life for Bilan, with women and children pulling up buckets of rather dirty-looking water, goats clustering round to get a sip of any water slopped over, and flies. Lots of them.

A and C are just fantasy. B is correct. The dust cloud in the distance is already growing as another truck approaches. Before setting off into potentially lethal desert, the villagers did the sensible thing. They said where they were going, how and when they would be getting back, and made sure that there would be someone to rescue them if things went wrong.

Fatiima and Assalama say the Tuareg encampment isn't far, just a couple of hours up the valley. You can load your water bags and gear onto their donkey.

A wadi is a dried-up desert valley. But it's not like that all of the year. The Sahara desert doesn't get much rain, but it does get some. And quite often much of that all falls in the winter at once. The result is sudden "flash" floods. With little vegetation to soak up the water, it just runs off the land, each rivulet joining up until quickly there's a raging torrent surging down the wadi, washing away whatever gets in the way, loose rocks and soil, bushes, houses, livestock (sometimes whole herds of goats at a time), and people....

Like the explorer Isabelle Eberhardt. Swiss by birth, she explored North Africa (Algeria) in the early twentieth century, mostly on horseback, sometimes with her Arab husband. As it wasn't acceptable for women to venture off alone, she would often dress up as a man on her adventures (she apparently passed off this bluff so easily because she was very skinny and rather hairy). She survived the heat and dust and the dehydration but, bizarrely, was killed by water and drowned in a sudden flash flood after a rainstorm in 1904.

There is also a story of a sudden flood saving an explorer's life — and not by providing drinking water, which is what you would expect. In 1854, the German explorer Heinrich Barth's caravan was under attack from Tuareg raiders. They were camped in a wadi, which started to flood, leaving the camp an island in the center of a huge muddy torrent, one that Barth reckoned would have been forceful enough to sweep a camel away. That stopped the Tuaregs attacking, but now there was another danger. As the river rose higher and the edges of his island started to collapse, it looked like Barth and his group were going to survive death at the hands of the Tuaregs only to be swept away by the newly formed river. Luckily, the water subsided. Barth was able to escape both the freak flood and the Tuaregs.

You set off shortly after sunrise. That way you'll hopefully arrive before it gets really hot. Of course it would have been cooler to go before dawn, but the two girls were scared of snakes called kraits that live in the wadi. In the light it is also easier to avoid the clumps of dried grass whose hooked burr seeds stick to your legs and irritate your skin. Getting them off seems next to impossible. They attach to your hands.

Their hooks break off under your skin and are very uncomfortable.

SAND GROUSE

You haven't been walking long when you flush out some dumpy pigeon-like birds with needle-pointed tails. These are sand grouse. They can be a good indication that water is near, since they need to drink regularly to help them digest the thousands of minuscule grass seeds that they pick off the earth each day. When sand grouse find a drinking pool, they even go as far as dipping themselves so that special moisture-absorbent feathers soak up the water. Then they take their precious cargo back to their chicks to give them a drink. If you see sand grouse flying low and in a straight line early in the morning or evening, they are probably flying to water. Remember that.

Signs of water

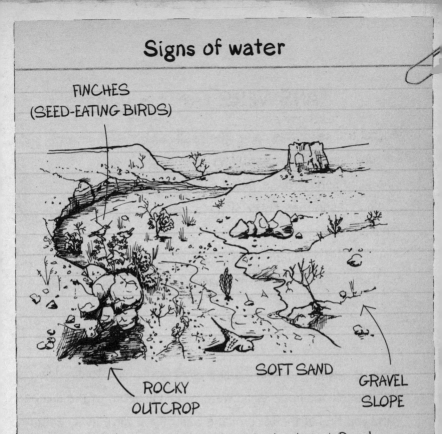

FINCHES
(SEED-EATING BIRDS)

ROCKY
OUTCROP

SOFT SAND

GRAVEL
SLOPE

Wadis are good places to find water in the desert. People living there often look at the lay of the land for the best places to dig down for it: sudden twists in the river bed or changes in rock type where underground water might build up, lines of vegetation, and animal trails all could indicate where water is located.

Look at this picture of the wadi. What signs are there that water is nearby? Where might be a good place to dig down into the earth for an improvised well?

Answers on page 54

ANSWERS from page 53

- Animal tracks (in this case, goats) all come together at the valley bottom. Maybe there was water here not long ago.
- Finch and sand grouse. Good signs that water is close.
- The bushes in the center of the wadi must be getting their water from somewhere.
- A kink in the river bed close to some outcrops of hard rock. The soft sand nearby is the first place you should start looking.

If there is water to find, it's likely you would have to dig down with a stick and hope some water would leak out of the damper sand you find at the base of the wadi. If you were lucky enough to find water on the surface, remember animals will have found it before you. This won't be a clear, fresh pool, but a soggy bog of goats' footprints and dung. Purify it, filter it, and use your iodine (see Chapter 1) before you consider drinking it.

But it's months since it last rained, so where does the water come from?

Aquifers!

In a wadi there is often a layer of hard rock that doesn't let water through it, not far under the surface. When the flash floods subsided, though most of the water evaporated in the heat, some soaked into the stream bed, sunk down as far as the non-porous rock, and stayed there. Digging down — sinking a well in the bottom of the wadi — would get you to that water.

There is subterranean water like this scattered all over the Sahara, trapped in cracks and fissures here and there, some in great underground lakes. Some of it's been there for millions of years. They call it fossil water. There have been various plans to pump up the water from the great aquifers and irrigate the desert to grow crops — but the cost would be enormous. It hasn't been done yet. Even where engineers have drilled down to the water table — as the layer of non-porous rock is called — and then pumped up water to the villages on the surface, the results have not always been as good as the engineers hoped. Many people in the Sahara have traditionally been nomadic, traveling with their camels and goats to where there was good grazing. The discovery of oil in many areas of the Sahara brought in money. Some of this was used for drilling small wells and putting in pumps. With lots of pumped water on tap, people settled in fixed villages. There, the goats and camels ate their way through all the good plants around the settlements. The result was that animal herding was no longer an option as a way of life in those areas. There's also been the problem that the water pumped up doesn't get replenished very often, as there's so little rain. After a few good years with plenty to drink, the water often runs out.

The Tuareg are camped in a narrow sub-valley that branches off from the main wadi. There's a scattering of acacia bushes and a much-trampled "water hole" that several dromedaries — one-humped camels — cluster around. Close by are three tents made of brush wood frames with cloth tied over the top. The walls of two of the tents, you notice, are made out of large, flattened cardboard boxes.

FATIMA AND
ASSALAMA

Sitting on the ground in front of one tent are two men covered entirely in blue robes with turbans wrapped around their heads and over their faces so that only their eyes show.

They show little reaction to your arrival. Were they expecting you?

Fatiima gestures for you to sit with them and take the silver cup of mint tea that you are offered. She will translate as you get down to the business of negotiating your passage across the great sand erg to the rock paintings of the Ahaggan plateau.

As you sip your tea, you can't help thinking there's something sinister about these two Tuareg facing you. Everyone knows the Tuaregs' fearsome reputation as desert raiders. And these two men won't even lower the veils that cover their faces?

Can they be trusted?

Will they take you across the erg? And will they bring you back?

Chapter 5

THE BLUE PEOPLE OF THE VEIL

"Of course, you'll have to buy a camel first," Ahmed says from under his blue face wrap. "And then there will be food and a guiding fee. We will, after all, have to make a detour from our regular route, and that will mean carrying more food and water, which in turn will mean taking more camels."

So far neither he nor his companion Abdullah have shown their faces. Even when sipping their tea they drink it under the cloth or cover their mouths with a hand to prevent you seeing them. Business seems, however, to be progressing fine. Tomorrow Ahmed and Abdullah plan to set off with a small caravan of camels — just twenty or so — ferrying slabs of rock salt to a village somewhere south of the Ahaggan plateau. They are quite happy to take you to a group of steep rock gorges in the Ahaggan where ancient rock paintings are to be found. Unfortunately, they don't know of the waterfall you talked about, though, never having explored the treacherous terrain of the Ahaggan themselves, they are willing to keep an

open mind that it exists. The deal is that you buy one of their camels. No, don't worry, you don't have to know the "ins and outs" of camel buying. They'll choose the camel and they'll buy it back from you at only a slightly lower rate once the trip is over — provided that it survives.

Their families have been traveling the desert to trade beyond the Ahaggan for generations, though in times past the camel caravans were often much larger — five hundred camels or more. From an early age, they've been taught how to navigate across seemingly featureless desert by "reading the land," looking for landmarks like the odd withered tree and observing the position of the stars. Traditionally, their caravans took weighty slabs of rock salt to the south and came back with gold or sometimes millet (grain). Sometimes, long ago, they brought slaves with their caravans, and they also did rather well by raiding other tribes' caravans (that's how they got their warlike reputation).

Timbuktu, René Caillié, and the Towers of Gold

There were several great centers for all this trans-Saharan trade, Koumbi Saleh, in Mauritania, and Agadez, in Niger. None were as famous as Timbuktu.

In modern-day Mali, at the southern fringes of the Sahara, on the Niger River, Timbuktu was the final destination for many of the North-South Caravans, a wealthy city with bazaars, universities, gold-plated minarets, and rulers who had more money than they knew what to do with. At least, that's what people in faraway Europe thought and they figured, if there was a profit to be made, then they should be the ones making it. There was just one problem, or rather two: the vast desert and the tribes that controlled it. As if crossing the vast Sahara weren't difficult enough, any European would face certain death if caught trying.

Enter René Auguste Caillié, a young Frenchman from a poor background with little education but an insatiable desire to be an explorer. By the age of twenty, he had been to West Africa twice and earned a small amount of money to finance his trip to Timbuktu. He knew that if he became the first European to get there (and back) alive, he would win a prize of 10,000 French francs from the Geographical Society of Paris. Not surprisingly, given that the locals were into killing any Europeans who passed that way, he went in disguise. Dressed as an Arab, he said he was an Egyptian who had been taken to Europe as a slave in his childhood; that was to explain why his Arabic was less than perfect. Shaky though his cover story was, it worked, despite various close shaves ...

TIMBUKTU & TRADE ROUTES

- He nearly died of scurvy (all the skin peeled off the roof of his mouth) and was nursed back to health by a kind woman who did not betray his identity.
- When he was caught collecting seeds on a barren hillside, he argued they were for use as medicine for a friend. His captors weren't convinced, but they let him go.
- When he was caught writing his diary (in French), he claimed to be writing songs and gave a quick rendition to the official that had detained him. Two verses were enough for the poor man who soon left without asking any more awkward questions.

And Timbuktu — did it live up to the hype? No way. It was just a has-been town of crumbling mud buildings. There were no gold-plated spires. Like the rest of the town they were made of mud, but with sticks sticking out of them to hold the mud in place. Caillié was unimpressed. He joined a caravan of 1,200 camels going north with lots of slaves. When he finally arrived at Rabat in Morocco, the French Consul there refused to accept his story because he was so scruffy, so he had to carry on to Tangier, where at last his outlandish tale was believed and he was sent home to Paris to receive his prize.

CAILLIÉ SINGING HIS WAY OUT OF TROUBLE

The building of roads and coming of trucks that can carry more salt faster than camels really affected the lives of the desert nomads. Fortunately for Ahmed and his band of Tuareg, there are still places where the trucks can't reach and a camel is the only good means of transportation. The nomad life still lives on.

And why do they keep their faces covered? The Tuareg call themselves *Kel Tagelmoust*, "the people of the veil." Traditionally they believe that covering the mouth keeps out evil spirits (women don't wear veils). Keeping the mouth covered is a sign of respect and politeness.

And the blue robes? That's tradition. Often the indigo dye leaches out and stains their skin. Sometimes the Tuareg are called the "Blue people" and sometimes they are called "The Abandoned of God." The name Tuareg was said originally to have been an Arab insult for these people whom the Arabs considered godless and wild.

WRAPPING A
TAGELMOUST
TURBAN

Choosing your camel

WHO NEEDS ALL-TERRAIN WHEN YOU'VE GOT ONE OF THESE?

Numerous special features to cope with all the extremes of the desert.

But before we start, just what do you know about the "ship of the desert"? Answer **true** or **false**.

1. Camels' wide feet allow them to stand on soft sand without sinking in far.
2. A camel's hump stores water.
3. Camels don't need to drink. Like many other desert animals, they can get all the moisture they need from the plants they eat.
4. Camels can't die of thirst.
5. Camels have long eyelashes to keep out sand and dust.
6. The only place where wild dromedaries (one-humped camels) live is in the deserts of Australia.
7. Camels can close their nostrils to keep out sand and dust.
8. Some Saharan camels have two humps.

Answers on page 68

Here are some more amazing camel design features:

- Large size allows them to absorb heat without overheating. They release the heat slowly when it's cooler.
- Coarse, insulating fur on top to prevent overheating.
- Less fur underneath so heat can radiate out.
- Ability to operate at high temperatures that would simply kill many other creatures.

Available in all Saharan and Middle Eastern deserts near you!

Fantastic range of funky desert colors — white/sandy, sandy brown, dark brown, and even skewbald brown and white (these animals often have a genetic mutation that makes them deaf).

Free: Spitting option. Spits out gunky, green slime when annoyed. [Please note: This feature is not optional. It is part of the package, as is the renowned evil temper. Actually, they most often get annoyed when you force them to get up and walk when they would rather be sitting on the ground resting.]

Water feature. Camels tend to pee over their back legs. This unpleasant habit is actually useful to the camel because the urine evaporates, taking away heat and cooling the camel down.

Once you've made your purchase, you're going to need the kit to make it all run smoothly. Here are some of the extras you'll require.

SADDLE & GUIDE ROP

- **Saddle.** This is made of wood, so you might need to pad it.
- **Guiding rope** (called a *teresum*) tied to a ring in the camel's right nostril. You steer your mount by a combination of pulling this string and treading down with your feet to apply pressure to its neck.

GUERBAS

- **Guerbas.** Goat-skin water bags. If you can dip the outsides in water before you set off, the water will slowly evaporate; this will help keep the water in the bag cooler.

An alternative (often easier to get hold of) water carrier is to use old inner tubes from truck tires. Cut in half and tie at the ends. Hang one water tube on each side of your camel to balance its load.

HALF-TIRE WATER CARRIER

· **Trail rations.** This is what the Tuareg take with them:
  · Zummita ground millet (a type of grain a bit like corn).
    You can mix it with water or camel's milk to make a
    paste or porridge or you can flatten it into "biscuits."
  · Dried dates.
  · Strips of paper-thin dried camel meat. The Tuareg
    sometimes dangle these from the saddles of the
    camels they are riding. They look a bit like brown,
    lacy paper doilies.

So here he is. Your fantastic purchase. You've decided to call
him "Cuthbert." Ahmed suggested the name of a well-known
make of 4-wheel-drive vehicle as this might inspire him to go
better over the rough terrain ahead, but as you thought this
was silly, you came up with the first name that came into
your head.

The deal is done. Tomorrow, you,
Cuthbert the camel, and
around twenty
more of his
friends and
relations will
set out across
the dunes.

ANSWERS from page 64

1. True. The weight is spread over a larger area, so the pressure on the ground is low.

2. False. It stores fat. The fat converts into water as the camel needs it. Look at the hump at the end of a long journey; it will be flopping to one side as the reserves get used up.

3. False. Camels have to drink regularly, though not as often as most other mammals. In summer, they can last five days or so before needing to fill up, but when they do, they can take in enormous quantities of water in a very short time — 100 liters (22 gallons) in ten minutes.

4. False. In the 1980s thousands of the Tuaregs' camels died because of a long drought.

5. True.

6. True. The camels in Australia are the descendants of animals used by explorers in the nineteenth century. There are no truly wild dromedaries anywhere else.

7. True.

8. False. The only camel with two humps is the Bactrian camel, which lives in the deserts of East Asia.

Chapter 6
ACROSS THE GREAT SAND SEA

One week out from the wadi and the days all seem to merge into one. Endless flat reg, and boulder-strewn hammada with virtually no plants, no landmarks, and no change of scenery to show you've actually made any headway in all those hours of traveling. For silent hours on camelback, you gently sway back and forth with Cuthbert's measured pace. There is no sound except the leathery creak of the saddles' harnesses and the camels' gentle footfalls on the gritty ground. Each day follows the same routine.

Camel caravan daily diary (could be any day — they're all very much the same)

Dawn. Get up. Morning prayer toward Mecca — east (Ahmed and Abdullah are Muslims).

Drink weak, syrupy tea. Eat breakfast — so far this has not varied from some *zummita*, millet porridge, and a blob of smelly dried fish moistened with camel's milk.

After breakfast. Ahmed and Abdullah, not so ably aided by you, round up the camels. If there are plants for them to eat, they will have been to left to forage. Sometimes the camels scatter quite a long way from the camp and it can take hours to fetch them all back. It's more convenient (for you, though pretty miserable for the camels) when there's no vegetation and they are given dry fodder (sacks of dry grass which you have to carry with you) because then they have their tied legs together so they can't go far.

Rest now and check the loads. Set off. The hours pass by slowly. Up on your camel, you're in a world of your own.

The terrain is mainly featureless. Even when there are rocks or dunes ahead, your progress feels so slow; the scenery doesn't change very often. There's often a stiff wind blowing and because of this it's usually too difficult to keep a conversation going with your guides. You wrap up your face in your tagelmoust turban and think through all the things you've ever done, or sing songs, to while away the time.

Noon. Stop. Unload camels and let them loose to forage again. More prayers, more tea. Lunch — some zummita and some dates, followed by a few hours' rest, which is just as well because by then it is really, really hot and you don't feel like doing anything else.

Mid-late Afternoon. Round camels up (same problems as described before) and go on until after dusk.

Evening. More prayers. Dinner. This meal is bigger and better than breakfast or lunch. You get some camel or goat meat, camel's milk, and more dates.

Night. Sleep on sand, wrapped in blanket. Don't sleep too close to the camels (or any nearby bushes) in case the ticks which feed on their blood decide you make a better home.

Dawn. Start again.

You've noticed that for the last couple of days you've been skirting along the edge of a sandy area with high dunes. That must be the edge of the sand sea *erg* that your map shows. According to your compass, Ahmed's route seems to be taking you out of your way. When you mention your concerns, he says not to worry. It's easier than traveling on the soft sand and besides, in the erg there will be no food for the camels — it's best to cross it at its narrowest point. How does he know where that is in this featureless flatness? He says he just knows. He's been here many times before. Sure enough, when you reach a *hammada* of orange boulders whose outsides have half cracked off in the heat to reveal purplish stone underneath, Ahmed signals for the caravan to turn toward the South. Your journey across the great sand sea of Najmer has begun.

To begin with, the change of scenery is a welcome relief, but as you thread your way over and around the great dunes that face you, the novelty wears off. Once again you're lost in that quiet world of inner contemplation as the camels plod on.

As the dunes rise higher and higher, the camels' progress gets slower. Sometimes they sink knee-deep in the soft sand. So do you, Ahmed, and Abdullah, when you dismount to urge the animals forward. You have to be particularly careful on the downward slopes where dune faces can slip away, taking camels with them and snapping the ropes that tether them together. Soon you just wish you could get back to the boring but easy-to-travel flat reg plains.

Ask someone to describe a desert and the chances are they'll mention sand dunes. In fact only around a seventh of the Sahara is covered with sand. The rest is gravel plain *reg* or rocky *hammada*. The sand grains in these *ergs* are nearly constantly moving, not so much rolling but bouncing. The wind picks up grains from the surface

and when they land they bash into other grains, causing them to bounce along, too. The leeward (downwind) side of a

BOUNCING SAND GRAINS

dune is called the slip face. It's always around the same steepness (thirty-two degrees from the horizontal), which is the steepest it can be before it naturally starts to slide. Sometimes you can hear the faint hissing of the windblown sand bouncing down the slip face and sometimes when you tread on it, it squeaks or groans as vibrations pass between the particles.

Sand Dune Quiz

Sand dunes can measure from just a few meters to up to hundreds of meters tall. There are many different shapes. These depend on how much sand is being blown and on the wind direction. On the next pages are some common sand dune shapes. Can you figure out which conditions caused them to form like this?

Type of dune	How it is formed
1. Barchan	A. The wind blows in line with the dune, building up jagged knifelike crests up to 200 meters high. Chains of these dunes end to end can go on for many kilometers.
2. Transverse	B. The wind blows across the dune like lots of barchans joined together as there is more sand available.
3. Seif – sword	C. Wind blows from several directions. These dunes tend to grow upward rather than being moved along.
4. Star	D. Sand domes form in the direction of the wind. Large ones may have long seif dunes on top.
5. Whaleback	E. Not much sand available. The wind blows across the dune at right angles so you get an even crescent shape.

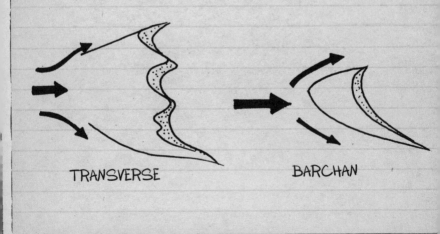

TRANSVERSE   BARCHAN

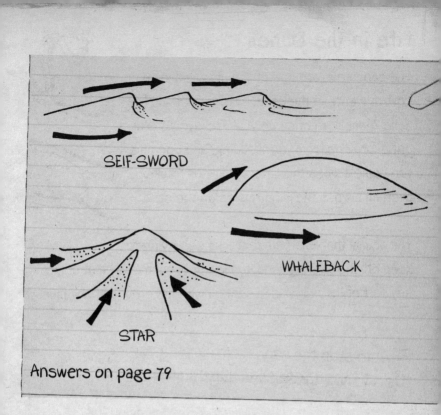

SEIF-SWORD

WHALEBACK

STAR

Answers on page 79

Dunes often start when sand collects around obstacles like bushes or rocks. Sand builds up, and over time the whole dune moves in the direction of the wind. In some places in the Sahara it is a fact of life that villages get covered over by moving dunes. The people move out, build new houses for a while, then dig out their old properties when the dune moves on and uncovers them.

Life in the Dunes

The sand seas are one of the most extreme environments in the desert, but animals do live here. More than once on your trek, you shake out scorpions from your bedding, and one time you come across this strange set of tracks overlaid across the wind ripples on the sand.

The animal that made these tracks was trying to keep off the burning sand, by moving in such a way that only a tiny part of its body was in contact with the ground at any time.

How to stop the sand from burning you.
Decide how these sand dune animals do it.

Animal	How it stops the sand burning
1. Fennec fox	A. Side-winding motion of body. Ripples its whole body forward, touching only two points on the sand at a time.
2. Skink (a lizard with shrunken legs)	B. Fur-covered soles to its feet.
3. Fringe-fingered lizard	C. Runs in short bursts, then sprints for its shady burrow when things get too hot.
4. Horned viper	D. "Swims" just under the sand's surface, where it's much cooler.

ANSWERS on page 80

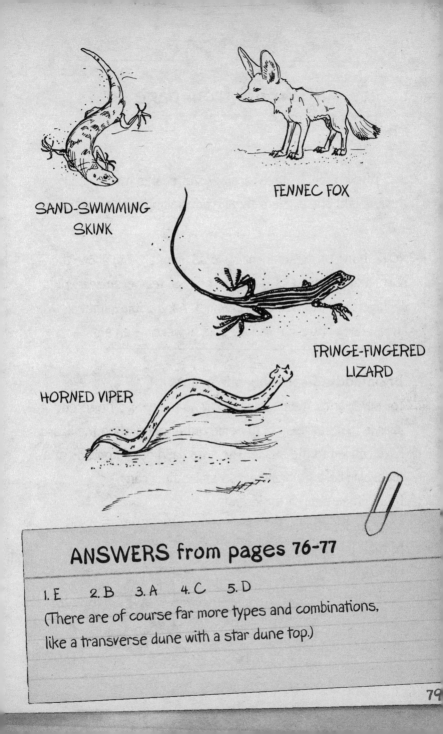

SAND-SWIMMING
SKINK

FENNEC FOX

FRINGE-FINGERED
LIZARD

HORNED VIPER

ANSWERS from pages 76-77

1. E   2. B   3. A   4. C   5. D
(There are of course far more types and combinations,
like a transverse dune with a star dune top.)

ANSWERS from page 78

1. B
2. D
3. C (the finger "fringes" are rows of scales that spread their weight and prevent them from sinking in the soft sand)
4. A

NOTE. None of these animals would hang around above the surface in the heat of the day. The high temperatures would damage their internal body chemistry and could kill them. One animal does brave the midday sun, however — an ant.

Brain-addled sprinting silver ants

For silver ants, the best way to avoid the fringe-fingered lizards that eat them is to come out at noon when the lizards have retired to the shade. The ants dash out, hundreds at a time, clambering up any grass stalks they can find in their search for insect corpses to drag back to their burrow. They have to be quick because soon their brains will start to overheat, making them forget the way back. Silver ants have been timed spending up to thirty minutes away from their holes in the heat of the day and in that time can cover many meters of ground. For their size, they are the fastest animals on Earth — and wouldn't you be, too, if you knew your brain was going to fry if you spent too long outside?

Day three on the erg. A wind has sprung up, sending a mist of sand grains bouncing up to around knee height. There is a strange static tingle to the air, and the hot gusts are spooking your camels who, in turn, are snorting, bellowing, and pulling away from Abdullah, who has dismounted and is walking in front. The sky is darkening, and your two guides, veils wrapped almost totally over their faces, are forcing the camels to sit down. A great cloud of brown is rolling toward you.

SANDSTORM!

Chapter 7
SANDSTORM

The sandstorm is coming. Already the first flurries of dust and grit are whipping around you. Any exposed skin stings with the scouring it's getting and, despite the glasses and the scarf wrapped over your face, your eyes are streaming and feel full of grit. You need to find shelter, but there is none on the open dune. Perhaps the slip face of the dune, slightly out of the wind, is a better place to sit out the storm. As the sky turns brown around you and the sand-blasting really starts, your biggest danger is getting separated from your group.

The camels are sitting down with their backs to the wind. Electrical sparks fly off their tails and crackle in the oven-blast air as static builds up and tries to jump to the ground. Once a spark like this blew up a bus whose driver was filling it up with fuel just before a sandstorm hit. A spark leaped from the fuel nozzle, igniting the flammable liquid. Luckily, the passengers had felt the static buildup and piled off the bus in the nick of time.

As the storm front rolls over you, Abdullah and Ahmed's main concern is to keep the camels together on the ground, and then to shelter themselves. Happily, the camels oblige, shutting eyes and nostrils. They are used to this. It would be tempting to squeeze next to Cuthbert to gain some shelter from the stinging sand. But what if he rolls over? He could easily squash you. So, you huddle with your two guides, wrapped up in a tarpaulin, buffeted by the maelstrom passing over you, slapped by facefuls of grit each time you lift the tarp to peer out and check how the camels are. You can feel the weight of sand building up on the windward side of your covering. You might have to move soon before you are buried.

The wind is lessening. The buffeting on the tarpaulin seems less frequent, and as you pull yourself upright you can see that most of the sand and dust is now below waist level and starting to settle. Ahmed is coaxing the camels to their feet — with lots of wheezing and groaning and snorting from them. While the caravan is made ready to carry on, you spare a second to look at yourself. You are covered head to toe in dust. Tears streak down your face where your eyes are streaming.

You, Ahmed, Abdullah, and twenty camels continue through the dunes. As you round one large dome, you catch a glimpse of this . . . an addax.

ADDAX

If ever there was an animal supremely adapted to life in the deep desert, then this is it.

Look at the picture. Can you think of some of the ways it is adapted? There are no clues to help you. If you've read about the jerboa in Chapter 3 and the camel in Chapter 5, you should have a good idea of the answers.

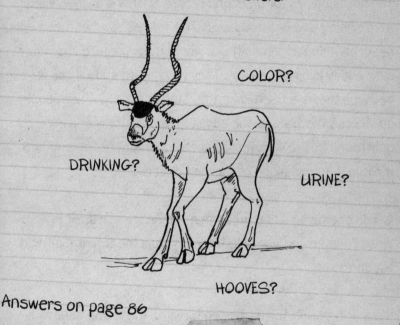

COLOR?

DRINKING?

URINE?

HOOVES?

Answers on page 86

· Doesn't need to drink. Gains all its moisture from the food it eats.
· Urine is very concentrated.
· Hooves are wide to spread its weight over soft sand.
· Light-colored to reflect sun's rays.

The addax stares for a second before sprinting away. Ahmed says seeing one is a good sign. The Tuareg say that these desert antelopes can sniff out good grass pasture and water over eighty kilometers away. They rarely hunt and kill addax because they are useful like this. Unfortunately, other people do. Across the Sahara, the addax is now critically endangered, only found in a few protected areas when once, not long ago, it roamed across much of the vast desert.

Could seeing an addax mean that the Ahaggan massif is close? Maybe you'll be able to see it from the top of that next big dune.

It's a tiring climb. For each step forward, the falling sand grains mean you slide back a short way. But the view you get from the summit makes the effort worth it.

The Ahaggan plateau. In the clear air you can see every detail; great cliffs and rock pinnacles rising out of the sand, colored bands of strata blasted by the wind, and sand-scoured overhangs. The scale is huge; you can tell from the pinpoint size of the addax that you can see at the base of the massif. Even your guides, Ahmed and Abdullah, seem impressed. Maybe there is water here after all, they concede. But in this vast pile of rocks, where will you look for it? Perhaps those two pin-tailed birds that you spot flying low over the sand towards the Ahaggan will give you a clue.

Quiz

1. What are the birds?
2. What does their flight tell you?
3. What directions should you give to your guides?

Decide what the answers are as you load up your camels and continue your trek into the "Pillars of the Ahaggan."

Answers on page 88

Chapter 8

THE PILLARS OF THE AHAGGAN

Ahmed is driving the camels at a fast trot as you near your destination. The cliffs stick up sheer above the sand. What did you realize when you saw the movement of the birds as you stood at the top of the dune?

ANSWERS from page 87

1. The birds are sand grouse.
2. Their low, direct flight means they are heading for water.
3. Tell Ahmed and Abdullah to follow the birds.

The walls of the canyon are high, vertical, and unclimbable, and for the first time in days you find yourself shaded from the sun. A finger of golden sand extends ahead of you as you walk the camels into the heart of the Ahaggan, its top layer crimson with dust eroded from a similarly colored band of rock that stripes across the cliffs fifty meters or so above. This stratum, like some others above and below, is clearly less resistant than the main rock of the Ahaggan. The wind and the grit it carries have scoured deep grooves and sculpted pillars, even arches in places along the rock walls. At the base of the cliff the wind has cut shady overhangs and hollowed-out shallow caves. These look to be great places to shelter if it weren't for the danger of rock falling from above. As if to confirm your doubts, some pebbles, perhaps blown by the wind, slip down one of the rock faces, their scratchy, tumbling pitter-patter echoing round the rock walls as they bounce their way down.

Dead end. The gap between the canyon walls has narrowed right down and is blocked with boulders. Maybe you were mistaken about the sand grouse flying this way. But no, there are signs of water. In a cleft at the top of the rockslide there is a straggly bush. And you can hear the chirruping of birds up there. You can see them now, small and buff-colored; they are hopping around the rocks by the bush. Maybe you could climb up there and explore further, if you left the camels here.

You are just considering your options when a sudden movement at the top of the rockslide catches your eye. What you see next is almost too quick to follow. A large cat-shaped animal launches itself from some shade nearby, and as the birds scatter, the cat swats one of them out of the air. For an instant you get a better view of the animal; it's Alsatian-dog-sized with tan fur, a short, stumpy tail, and long, tufted ears like a lynx. It's a caracal. By the time you've worked that out, it has hidden itself, you think, under a rock overhang by the top of the landslip.

Caracal, birds, a bush; the water must be beyond that boulder-slide.
This is what you see ahead of you. Can you figure out a safe way to clamber up?

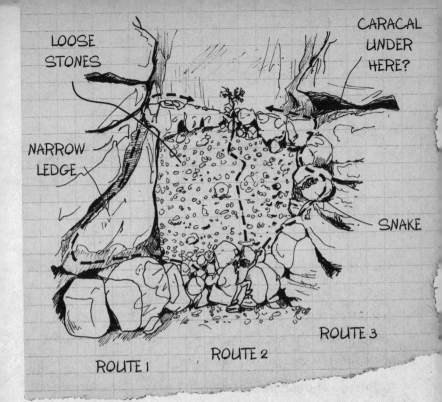

Route 1. Make your way up the narrow ledge that juts out of the left-hand side rock wall. There are handholds later on in that long deep fissure.

Route 2. Clamber up the boulders then across the loose gravel "scree" to the bush.

Route 3. An easy scramble up some rocks jutting out from the right-hand wall, but what about that snake basking in the sunshine on the rock? And even if you get past the snake, isn't that the overhang where the caracal is hiding?

Answer on page 95

You clamber up. The valley beyond is narrow and sheer-sided.
There are trees growing, gnarled old cypresses, perhaps
thousands of years old. Their cones and seeds litter the
canyon floor in places. None of the seeds has germinated
for hundreds of years. It is simply too dry. As you clamber up
further, you notice the colors in the rock overhangs are not
the splotchy colors of unusual rocks — these have been
painted on. You can make out shapes of human figures,
animals like hippos and giraffes, cypress trees — perhaps
the very same ones you have just passed. The pictures show
people herding black-and-white cattle through lush grasslands.

There are mountains there that you recognize as the Ahaggan, but their canyons hold rivers and forests. As you study the murals in more detail, you realize there are several different styles of art here, as if they've been painted at different times. Some, the earliest ones, show stick figures of hunters spearing antelope and zebra. Later, it appears the people settled down and farmed the land. There are other pictures, too, fewer in number. Some show chariots and battles. Others show camels and people dressed similarly to the Tuareg who brought you here. What do these pictures mean? Did the people in the pictures hunt all the animals and their cattle eat the grass? Did they turn the grassland into the desert we have now?

The answer is no. It's all to do with changes in the Earth's climate. Five thousand years ago, the Sahara received more rainfall than it does now. Animals and people prospered. Since then the climate dried out. The early farmers moved south and north, developing civilizations as they went. One group settled in the Nile Valley and eventually became the Ancient Egyptians. Over the centuries, the grassland became desert. That's not to say that people haven't made the situation worse in places. Much of North Africa close to the coast had forests until fairly recent historical times (many of the lions, elephants, and other exotic animals used by the Romans in their gladiatorial contests came from North Africa). But as the trees were cut down for wood, and goats and cattle overgrazed the areas, fertile land turned into barren desert. This is still happening all around the edges of the Sahara. It's called **desertification**. Trees are cut down, animals overgraze what's left, and then the topsoil blows away. This is one of the major reasons for poverty in the lands immediately to the south of the Sahara desert.

A tumble of gravel in the boulders ahead of you nudges you from your detailed study of the rock art. That looked distinctly like a small crocodile skittering through the dust under the cypress bushes. And isn't that a dragonfly? Aren't they always found close to water? Eagerly, you bound over the boulders of the canyon . . . and splash into **water**.

Shaded by the high walls of the canyon is a long, narrow lake. There are clumps of green grass and bushes growing at the sides, and hidden under a deep overhang you can just make out the eyes of a small crocodile sticking out just above the surface. Other animals come here; that's obvious from tracks in the sand close to the water. You can make out the hoof marks of mouflon mountain sheep and paw marks of caracal and striped hyena. There are birds here, too, finches and other seed eaters, insect eaters like pipits, and the falcons that hunt them. You have discovered an abundance of life in one of the harshest parts of the desert.

ANSWER from page 91

The Best Route?

All three routes are not without danger, but if you weigh it, the risk is from falling rather than from animal hazards.

Route 1. This might be easy enough to do, but if you slipped you would be hurt by the height of the fall. The handholds close to the top are prime scorpion or snake hiding places too.

Route 2. There is the chance of triggering off another rock fall. If you roll down with some of the large boulders, you could sustain crush injuries.

Route 3. The safest option, since the climb is all straight-forward — across rocks that will not fall. The snake will probably move away if you approach it and the caracal has got some food and is not dangerous in any case.

And the waterfall?

You find that at the far end of the ribbon of water. The word "waterfall" makes it sound grander than it really is. It's a cleft in the rock where subterranean water spills out of the cliff and tumbles down as a continuous shower into the soupier water of the oasis below. The spring water is cool, clear, and fresh, almost magical in this land of utter dryness.

You've made it!

And what a discovery! A cascade of the clearest, freshest water where none was suspected. What should you do now? Keep your discovery quiet so others won't come and spoil the paradise you've found or make sure that if others know about this magical place it has the protection it needs? You could write a book about your experiences in the desert and publicize it with television interviews. There'll surely be learned scientific papers to publish. And when you tell your story, remember that you didn't get here single-handedly. You needed the help of Mohamed with his truck (even if it did break down), his sisters, Fatima and Assalama, and finally Ahmed and Abdullah with their train of camels. And don't forget your own camel, Cuthbert. He didn't bite or spit at you once!

You can mention all this help when you tell your story — when you get home . . .

But, how will you get back? It will be a long journey, possibly fraught with as much hardship as the trip here. Look at this map of your route and work out the way you came. Which hexagons did you pass through in order?

· You set out from the oasis at Djella . . .
· Across the *reg* plains, where Mohamed's truck broke down.
· You stopped at the well at Bilan and walked up the wadi to the Tuareg encampment.
· Your camel trek took you first across the gravel plain *hammada* then . . .
· Across the sand *erg* of Najmer to . . .
· The Ahaggan massif.

Answer on page 100

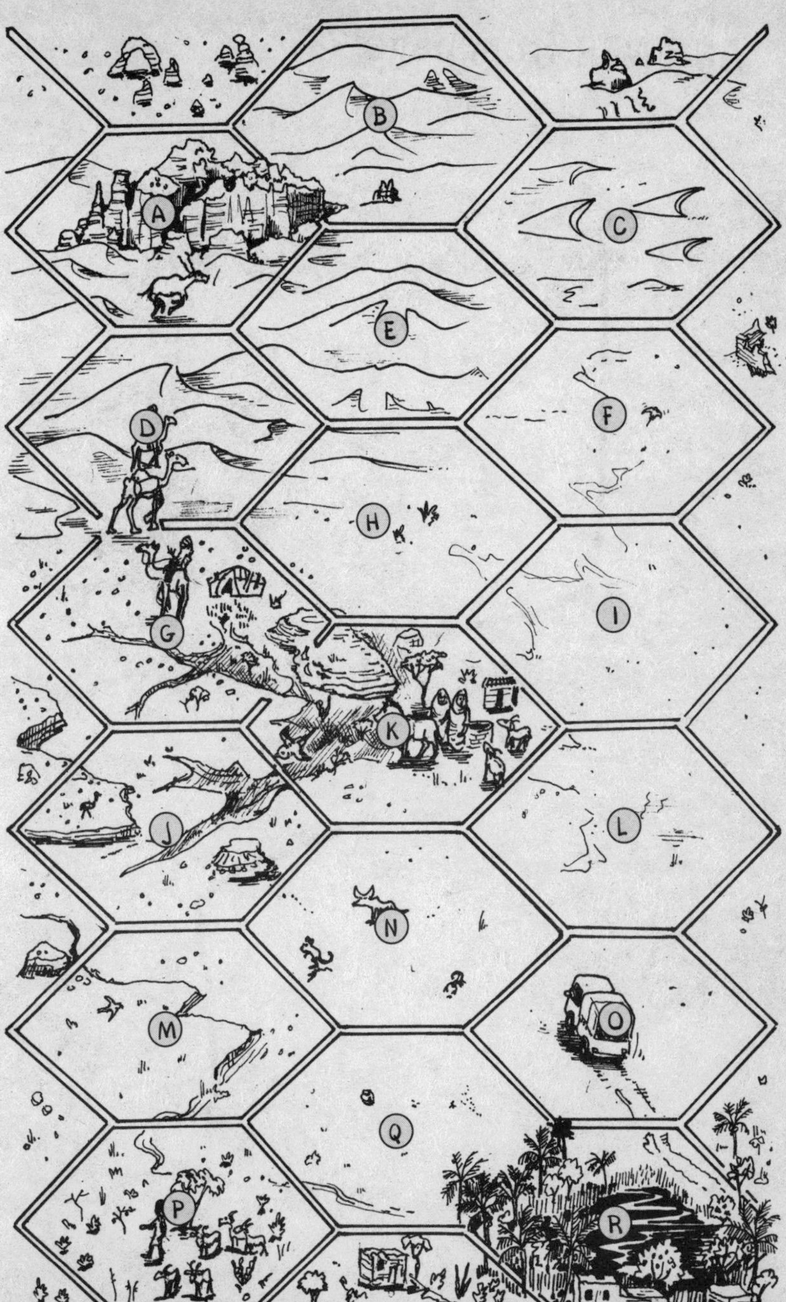

A
B
C
D
E
F
G
H
I
J
K
L
M
N
O
P
Q
R

You've proved yourself to be a skilled explorer of the Sahara desert, so what next? More deserts, or maybe you would like to branch out into different areas — like the **Arctic** wastes. You could climb the high **Himalayas** or set out across the **South Sea Islands**. Whichever one,

Explorers Wanted!

Your mission...

should you choose to accept it,
is to lead an expedition to Murrelet Island
to uncover the mystery of the lost airship *Italia.*

Are you ready for the challenge?

Explorers Wanted to:

- Face the deadly cold
- Handle a team of tough sledge dogs
- Survive thin ice and whiteouts
- Build an igloo
- Fend off ravenous polar bears

Includes the author's own expedition notes and sketches!

GREENLAND

3971 Qaanaaq
3970 Dundas

3964 Danmarkshavn

3962 Upernavik

3985 Constable Pynt
3980 Ittoqqortoormiit

3963 Niaqornat
3961 Uummannat
3952 Ilulissat
3953 Qeqertarsuaq
3951 Qasigiannguit
3950 Aasiaat

3910 Kangerlussuaq

Polarcirkel · Arctic Circle · Polarkreis
3911 Sisimiut
Qaarsahua Killeqarfia
3913 Ammassalik

3912 Maniitsoq

KALAALLIT NUNAAT
GRØNLAND
3900 NUUK 3905 Nuussuaq

SO...YOU WANT TO EXPLORE THE NORTH POLE?

You want to...

Drive a pack of huskies across the **frozen Arctic** wastes?

Fend off **polar bears** and packs of **ravenous Arctic foxes?**

Ski through the land of the midnight sun?
If the answer is **YES**, then this is the book for you.

Read on to learn the essentials of how to survive in this freezing land of snow and ice, how to cross the perilous ice floes, and how to navigate where the only direction you can go is south! Find out about the explorers who tried before you; some who succeeded and some who didn't make it, in this freezer at the top of the world.

Mission Dossier

Your mission is to find the lost "Airship *Italia*."

Timeline:

May 23rd, 1928.

Italian aviator General Umberto Nobile sets off northward in an airship from the Arctic island of Svalbard, his aim to cross the pole and investigate rumors that there are undiscovered land masses among the shifting ice floes.

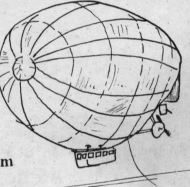

May 25th, 1928.
A distress signal was received:

"Too much weight of ice encrusting 'envelope' ... force down ..."

Radio contact was lost. An international rescue mission was set in motion. Seaplanes scoured the Arctic Ocean. Ice-breaking ships smashed their way through the pack ice and eventually Nobile and most of his crew were found (you can read what happened in Chapter 8). But neither the airship nor the six unfortunate Italians who were still on it when it blew away in the wind after it had crashed were ever discovered. What happened to them, nobody knows. Until now, that is ...

January: A satellite image has shown a long, dark shape on the ice, uncovered in the pack ice close to Murrelet Island, north of Greenland. Could this be the *Italia*? Your task is to go there and find out.

Warning: You have to act fast. By the time you get your expedition together it is late March. Soon the warming spring temperatures will be thawing the polar ice sheet, breaking it up. Then the ice carrying the airship — if that's what it is — will float off. You will have lost your chance to find it, possibly forever.

Where are you going?

The Arctic. The top of the world. It's extremely cold, bare, and windswept, and for the most part covered with snow and ice. Around the edges there is land like the huge mountainous islands of Greenland and Svalbard, but over the pole itself there is just ice. Made of frozen water, the ice cap's shape is constantly changing as its edges melt in

SUMMER IN THE ARCTIC CIRCLE

the summer and refreeze in the winter. Meanwhile, ocean currents ram the ice sheets together, endlessly splitting them apart and rejoining them in different ways. Virtually nothing grows here, and all life looks to the sea for food.

Further south, on the lands fringing the Arctic Circle, is the tundra, a wilderness of knee-high forests and mossy bog land. The tundra teems with life for two or three short months in the summer, and is frozen solid for the rest of the year.

The seasons are extreme. In the height of Northern summer there is continual daylight. With the tilt of the Earth on its axis, at this time of year, the northern part is always pointed toward the sun. On the ground, you see the sun dip but never go below the horizon. This is the time when the ice floes break up, the snow on the tundra melts, and birds like swans and geese migrate north to feed, before the days become shorter and the cold comes again. By Northern midwinter, the Arctic is smothered by continual darkness. Temperatures plummet and most of the animals and birds (that are able to) move south to survive.

ICE CAP SUMMER

ICE CAP WINTER

Of course, at the other end of the planet, the Antarctic, the same climatic switch happens, but the other way around.

Winter in the Arctic is summer in the Antarctic. While the north has continual night, the south has continual day — and vice versa in the Antarctic summer/Arctic winter.

But what other differences exist between life at the two poles? For a start, the Antarctic has a solid continental landmass underneath it. There are even desert valleys where no snow ever falls. But for the most part, covered with snow and ice, the two polar areas look the same. Many of the animals living at the ends of the Earth are similar. Some are the same, but there are differences.

ARCTIC TERN

BRÜNNICH'S GUILLEMOT

ARCTIC AND ANTARCTICA

Look at this picture. Choose whether the creatures live in the **north**, **south**, or **both**.

1. Polar bear
2. Seal
3. Walrus
4. Minke whale
5. Caribou
6. Emperor penguin
7. Brünnich's Guillemot
8. Arctic tern

So, what's it actually like in the Arctic?

Before you set off, you're going to need to know what the conditions are like …

Pack Ice. A flat expanse of dazzling white as far as you can see in all directions. The sun is low in the sky, casting your shadow out across the whiteness. A strong wind blows across you; the tiny crystals of ice it carries with it sting any exposed skin in the crisp coldness. Wrapped up in your down-filled coat and snow boots you feel warm enough, but in the back of your mind you know it wouldn't take much to tip the balance and turn this into a survival situation, one in which you wouldn't stand much chance of coming out alive.

Mission notes

Mission notes

Mission notes

Mission notes

Mission notes

Mission notes

About the author

Writer and broadcaster Simon Chapman is a self-confessed jungle addict, making expeditions whenever he can. His travels have taken him to tropical forests all over the world, from Borneo and Irian Jaya to the Amazon.

The story of his search for a mythical Giant Ape in the Bolivian rainforest, *The Monster of the Madidi*, was published in 2001. He has also had numerous articles and illustrations published in magazines in Britain and the United States, including *Wanderlust*, *BBC Wildlife*, and *South American Explorer*. He has written and recorded for BBC Radio 4 and lectured on the organization of jungle expeditions at the Royal Geographical Society, of which he is a fellow. When not exploring, Simon lives with his wife and his two young children in Lancaster, England, where he teaches high school physics.